Animals vs. Humans

# BIRDS SWARM

Heather Rook Bylenga

WWW.APEXEDITIONS.COM



Apex is distributed by North Star Editions:
sales@northstareditions.com | 888-417-0195

Produced for Apex by Red Line Editorial.

Photographs ©: iStockphoto, cover, 1, 12–13, 30–31, 39; Shutterstock Images, 4–5, 6–7, 8–9, 10–11, 14–15, 17, 18–19, 24–25, 26–27, 28–29, 32–33, 34–35, 36–37, 40–41, 42–43, 44–45, 46–47, 48–49, 50–51, 52–53, 54–55, 56–57; Frank C. Curtin/AP Images, 20–21; Steven Day/AP Images, 22–23; Red Line Editorial, 58–59

**Library of Congress Control Number: 2023922206**

**ISBN**
979-8-89250-208-5 (hardcover)
979-8-89250-229-0 (paperback)
979-8-89250-270-2 (ebook pdf)
979-8-89250-250-4 (hosted ebook)

Printed in the United States of America
Mankato, MN
082024

## NOTE TO PARENTS AND EDUCATORS

**Apex books are designed to build literacy skills in striving readers. Exciting, high-interest content attracts and holds readers' attention. The text is carefully leveled to allow students to achieve success quickly.**

# TABLE OF CONTENTS

Chapter 1
DANGER IN THE AIR 4

Chapter 2
ALL ABOUT SWARMS 9

That's Wild!
SICK IN THE SKY 16

Chapter 3
BIRD STRIKES 18

Chapter 4
CITY SWARMS 29

That's Wild!
CLEARING PIGEONS 38

Chapter 5
COUNTRY SWARMS 41

Chapter 6
FACING THE PROBLEMS 50

MAP • 58
COMPREHENSION QUESTIONS • 60
GLOSSARY • 62
TO LEARN MORE • 63
ABOUT THE AUTHOR • 63
INDEX • 64

Chapter 1

# DANGER IN THE AIR

In Seattle, a plane speeds down the airport runway. It takes off into the sky. Suddenly, a swarm of birds appears. Hundreds of starlings hit the plane. Some birds get sucked into the engines.

Most bird strikes happen when a plane is taking off or landing.

Passengers scream as the plane wobbles. The pilot must make an emergency landing. He steers the plane toward an empty field. The plane hits the ground hard, but it doesn't break. Some people are hurt. But everyone survives.

**A group of starlings is called a murmuration.**

## FATAL FLOCKS

Birds flying into planes can be deadly. In 1996, a plane was landing in the Netherlands. Hundreds of starlings and lapwings got sucked into the plane's engines. The plane crashed and caught fire. More than 30 people died.

Starling swarms can include up to 750,000 birds.

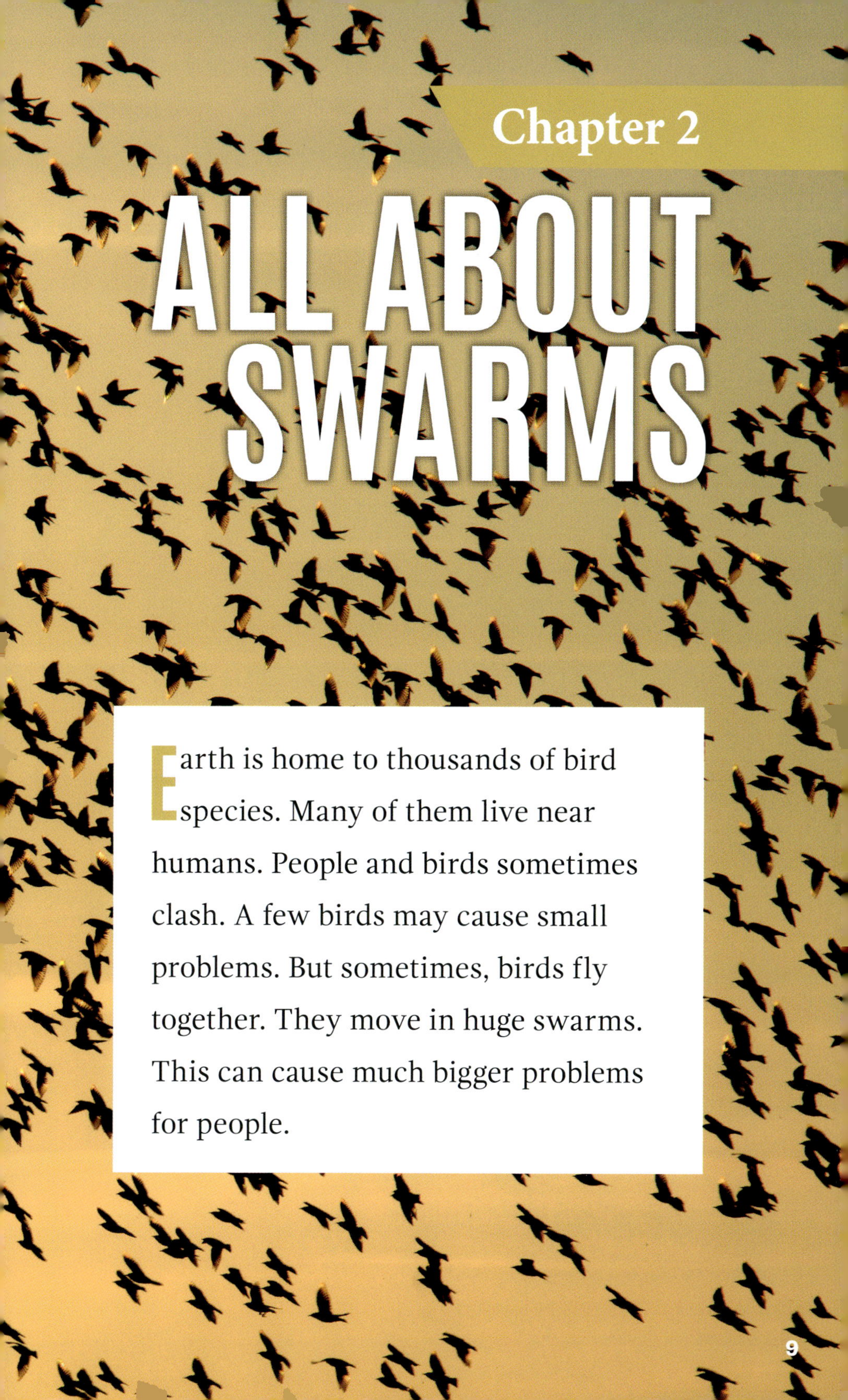

Chapter 2

# ALL ABOUT SWARMS

Earth is home to thousands of bird species. Many of them live near humans. People and birds sometimes clash. A few birds may cause small problems. But sometimes, birds fly together. They move in huge swarms. This can cause much bigger problems for people.

Birds fly in large groups for many reasons. It helps them stay safe. They can avoid predators. Other times, birds need new spaces to make nests. They may join up to search together. Or they can look for food and water. Birds may also migrate as a swarm. Flying in a group is less tiring.

Many birds fly together in a V shape. It helps them save energy.

## HOW A SWARM FLIES

Birds in a swarm move as one. Each bird carefully watches its neighbor. The birds move together in the same direction. That way, no birds bump into one another.

Trash from humans can harm bird habitats.

Many bird species have more birds now than ever before. But there are more humans, too. Humans often want to use the same land as birds. They build homes and businesses. They build roads. These actions may destroy bird habitats. Then, birds need to find new homes.

## MOVING FAR

When birds migrate, they travel long distances. The birds must stop to eat and rest. The birds might be noisy and messy in new areas. They may eat a lot of food. And they can spread diseases wherever they go.

House sparrows first came to New York in the 1850s. They sometimes take over the nests of native birds.

Humans make some bird issues worse. For example, humans brought sparrows and pigeons from Europe to North America. These birds competed with the native birds. They tried to use the same food and space.

Sometimes, new birds become invasive. They take over. Other animals may die out in an area.

## STARLING SPREAD

**In the 1890s, 100 starlings were released in New York. Starlings are smart. They got used to the city. These birds thrived and spread quickly. In 2023, about 200 million starlings lived in North America.**

## That's Wild!

# SICK IN THE SKY

In 1961, thousands of birds took over a California town. These birds were sooty shearwaters. They were sick and confused. They threw up fish blood. They fell from the sky. They slammed into buildings. For years, scientists didn't know why. In 2011, they figured it out. The birds were poisoned. Harmful domoic acid got into the birds' food.

**Domoic acid can come from algae. Small fish eat the algae. Then birds eat the fish.**

In 1963, Alfred Hitchcock made a famous movie. It was called *The Birds*. He was inspired by the California sooty shearwaters.

## Chapter 3

# BIRD STRIKES

Every year, millions of birds die from hitting cars. But the biggest disasters happen when birds hit airplanes. The term "bird strike" usually refers to that. Bird strikes cause more than $1 billion in damage each year. They have killed more than 250 people since 1988.

Up to 340 million birds die each year from getting hit by cars.

The worst bird strike in history happened in 1960. A plane tried to take off in Boston. The plane hit a flock of starlings. Some birds were sucked into the engines. The plane crashed in Boston Harbor. The plane broke into pieces. Luckily, 10 people survived. But 62 people died.

## MILITARY DISASTER

**In 1995 in Alaska, a military plane hit Canada geese. The plane had four engines. Birds flew into two engines on the same side. The plane crashed and exploded. All 24 crew members on the plane died.**

People removed the crashed plane from Boston Harbor. They put it back together to find out what happened.

Another famous bird strike happened in 2009. Minutes after takeoff, a plane in New York flew into a flock of Canada geese. Geese flew into both engines. The plane completely lost power. But the pilots kept the plane under control. They landed it on the Hudson River. They saved everyone on board.

## HELICOPTER CRASH

In 2014 in England, a helicopter was flying. A flock of geese smashed through the windshield. The pilots were knocked out. The helicopter crashed. All four people on board died.

The New York plane landing became known as the "Miracle on the Hudson."

More bird strikes are reported now than in the past. People keep better records. But also, some bird species have increased. Airplane travel has gone up, too. Birds usually fly away if they hear a plane nearby. But many new engines are quieter. New engines are also more powerful. They may be more likely to suck in birds.

## NEW PLANES, NEW PROBLEMS

Many new planes have only two engines. This means there is less backup if an engine fails. Often, new engines are built to take in birds without breaking. But it doesn't always work.

**Many bird strikes don't badly harm planes. But larger birds or flocks can cause more damage.**

Airports deter birds in different ways. Air cannons make loud sounds to scare birds. So do fireworks. Airports may also cut grass short. That makes it harder for birds to nest. Some airports use radar to track birds. But strikes still happen. More than 50 may occur each day.

## PIGS AND DOGS

Some airports use other animals to control birds. Salt Lake City uses pigs. They eat gull eggs. An airport in Michigan uses dogs. They chase snowy owls away.

Some birds are attracted to wide-open areas of grass at airports. So, airports may keep grass long or short in different seasons.

Delhi may have more than 100,000 black kites. The birds often eat from the city's landfill.

# CITY SWARMS

Sometimes, swarms of birds swoop down on cities. Thousands of birds may gather in one place. Swarms may come to cities looking for food. This happens in Delhi, India. Black kites swarm there. The city has factories that clean meat. Kites gather to collect extra meat bits that workers throw away.

Birds may also pass through cities as they migrate. Cities have many buildings. Those buildings offer good places to nest. So, some birds stay permanently. They adapt to city life. They find new food sources. They find material for nests.

Bright city lights can attract migrating birds.

## CHIMNEY ISSUES

Swifts migrate through California. In 2021, hundreds flew down a house's chimney. They invaded every room. Later, 1,000 swifts got stuck in the chimney of another home.

Bird swarms are often noisy and messy. But they can cause bigger problems, too. Bird poop can harm buildings. The droppings contain acids. These acids can break down stone. Sometimes bird poop even hurts a building's structure. For example, it can break down roof material. This can cause holes. The ceiling may start leaking.

## LOSING FEAR

**In some places, humans feed city birds. They give the birds seeds and crackers. This can attract more birds to the area. Birds may also stop fearing humans. They don't fly away. They stay and leave more droppings.**

Bird droppings can damage statues. Statues get weaker and change colors.

Diseases from birds may spread more in dirty or crowded areas.

Birds in cities can create health risks, too. Some birds have diseases. The birds' feathers and poop carry germs. People can get sick from touching the birds or being near them. Illnesses such as bird flu can be deadly. Another common illness is histoplasmosis. Many people recover if they get it. But others die.

## CLEANING SAFELY

Some people get sick from cleaning up bird poop. Wearing gloves can help. But germs from poop can also get into dust and air. Breathing in these germs is dangerous. Wearing masks helps people stay safe.

Starlings may rest on buildings and poles. City workers in Rome use sounds to scare them off.

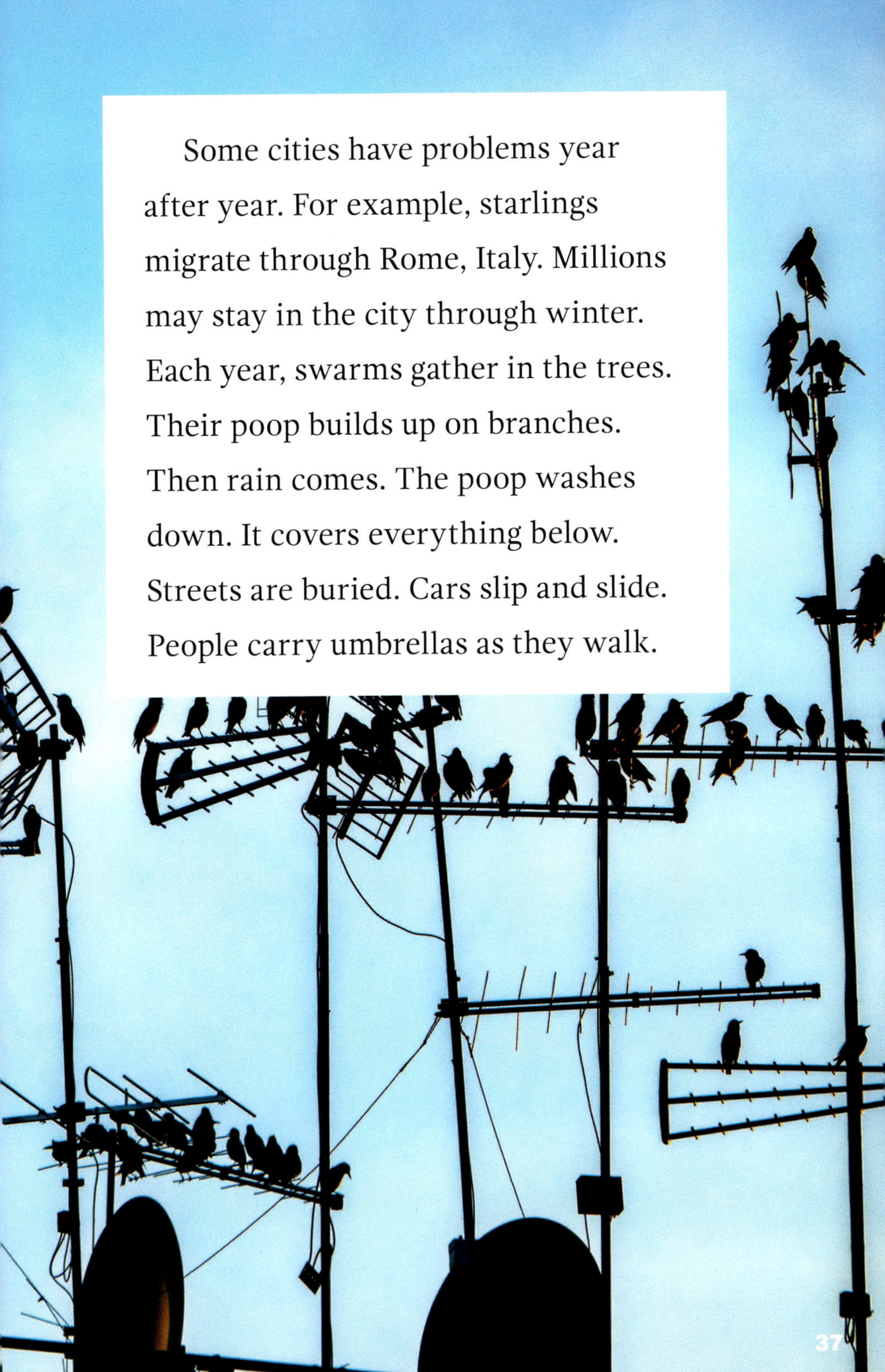

Some cities have problems year after year. For example, starlings migrate through Rome, Italy. Millions may stay in the city through winter. Each year, swarms gather in the trees. Their poop builds up on branches. Then rain comes. The poop washes down. It covers everything below. Streets are buried. Cars slip and slide. People carry umbrellas as they walk.

## That's Wild!

# CLEARING PIGEONS

For years, London had a pigeon problem. Swarms of pigeons lived in Trafalgar Square. Thousands could appear in the square at a time. In 2003, the city made a new law. No one could feed the pigeons. The city also brought in hawks. Hawks scared some pigeons away.

Some people complained about the change. But many people were happy. Trafalgar Square became cleaner. It was also less crowded with pigeons.

**Some people tried to save the pigeons. These groups wanted to make sure pigeons were not harmed.**

Grackles can cause a lot of damage. They eat many kinds of crops.

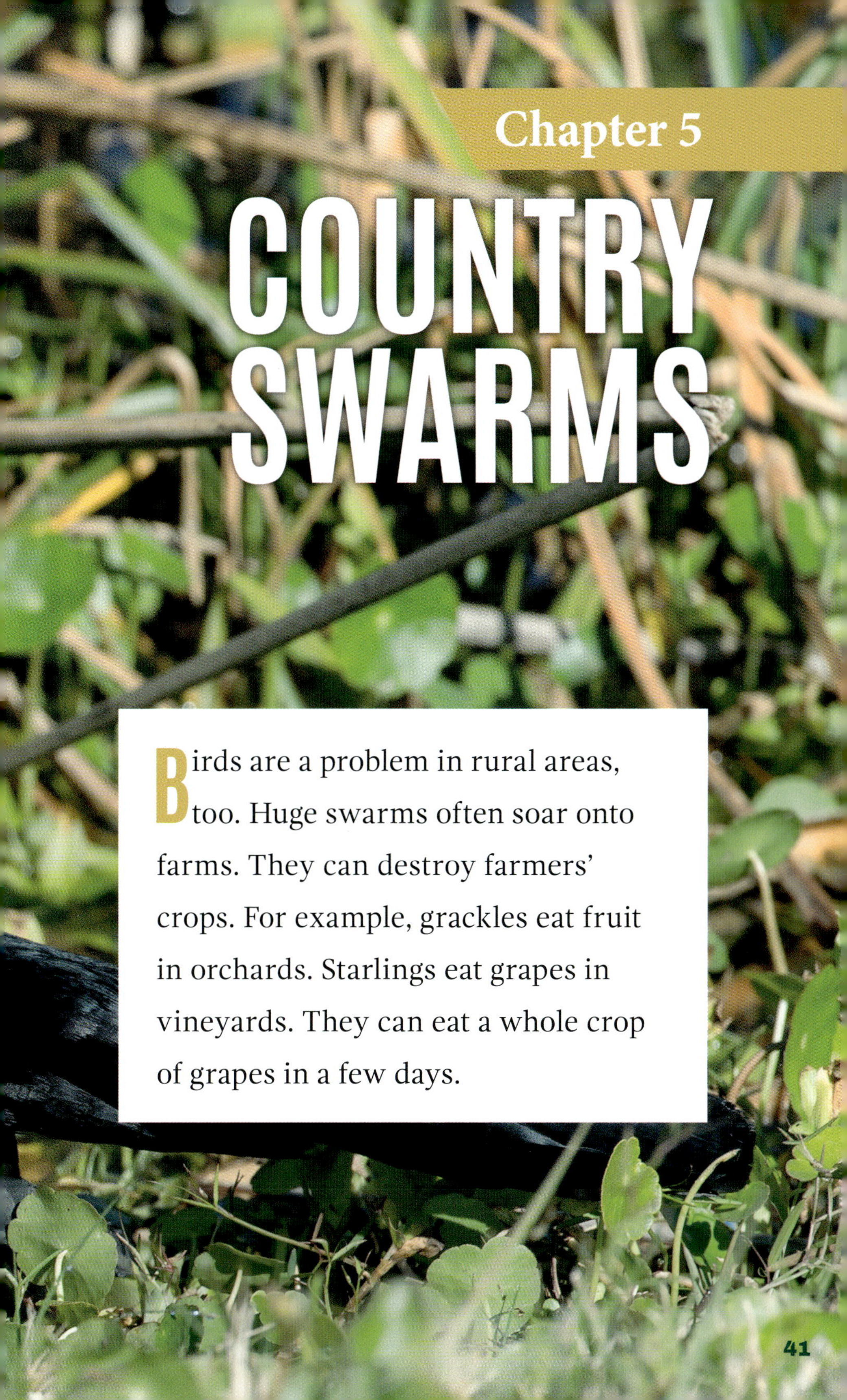

Chapter 5

# COUNTRY SWARMS

Birds are a problem in rural areas, too. Huge swarms often soar onto farms. They can destroy farmers' crops. For example, grackles eat fruit in orchards. Starlings eat grapes in vineyards. They can eat a whole crop of grapes in a few days.

## BIRD TO BIRD

Birds can spread diseases to other farm animals. When wild birds visit farms, they leave poop behind. Farm birds such as chickens might touch it. They can get diseases from the wild birds.

Blackbirds, crows, and cowbirds eat corn. Farmers may grow corn to feed their animals. And they may hope to sell some of it. So, losing corn costs farmers a lot of money. Losing other grains can be costly, too. In one day, 1,000 birds can eat 100 pounds (45 kg) of grain.

Birds may help crops grow by eating insects and rodents. But many birds eat crops, too.

Birds can also destroy farm equipment. For example, bird poop can break down metal in machines. It can fill up drains and vents. Bird droppings can also ruin barn roofs. Starlings sometimes build nests in tractor engines. When the tractors turn on, the engines heat up. Nests may catch fire.

## RAVEN POWER

**In 2016 and 2017, raven flocks roosted on Montana electrical towers. Swarms sat on power lines. Their droppings caused power failures. Later, workers put spikes on towers to keep the birds away.**

Starling nests may destroy tractors.

**Sometimes mosquitoes bite sick birds. Then mosquitoes may spread diseases such as West Nile virus to humans.**

Bird swarms near farms can cause water pollution. Bird poop can get into rivers or streams. Dirty water can spread to water sources people use. People can get sick.

Parasites are another risk. Tiny parasites live and feed on other animals. Swarming birds may carry parasites to farm animals.

## BAD CEREAL

**Pigeons often nest in machines that hold grain. Mealworms live in pigeon nests. So, mealworms can get into the grain. In the early 2020s, people found mealworms in breakfast cereals.**

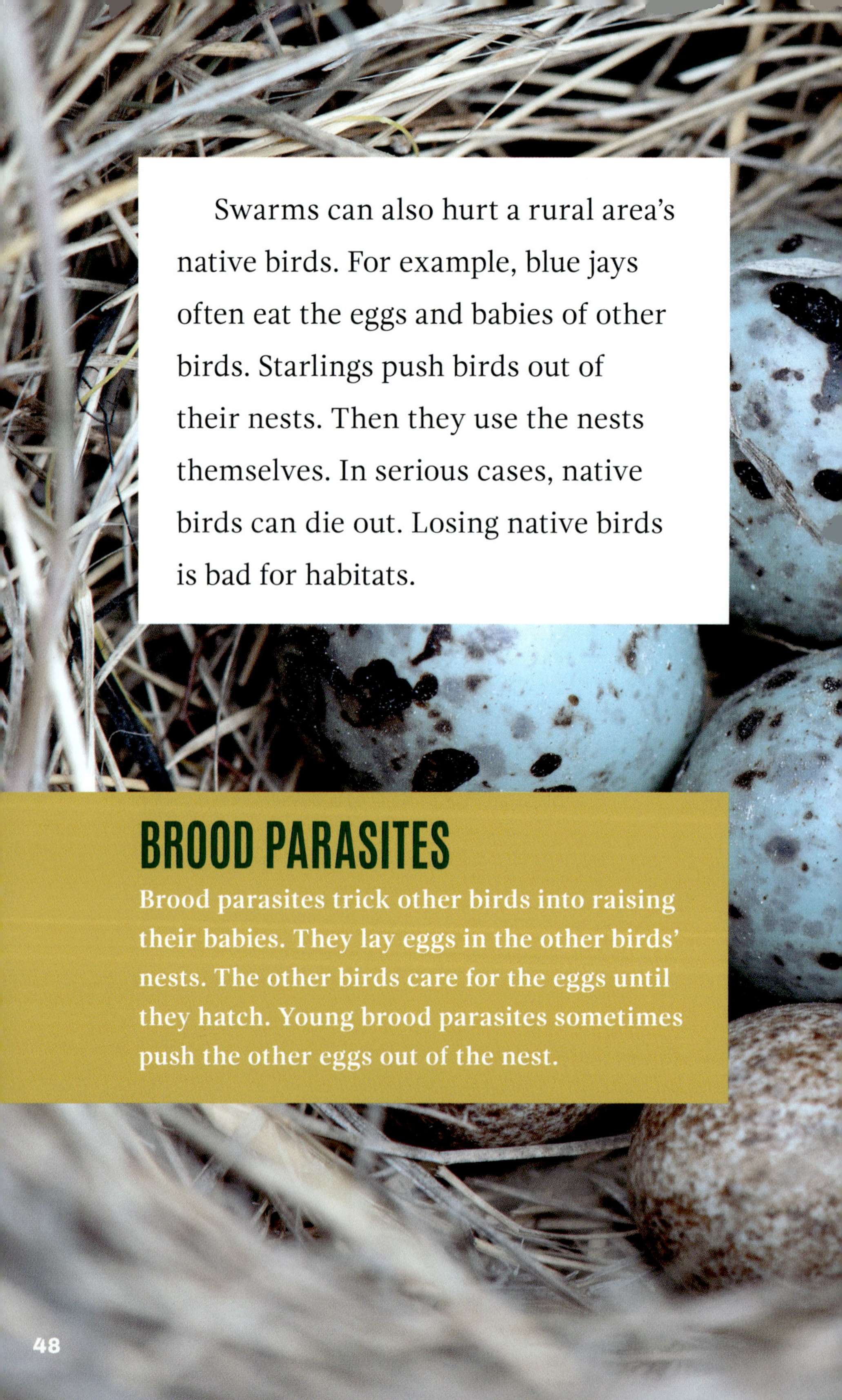

Swarms can also hurt a rural area's native birds. For example, blue jays often eat the eggs and babies of other birds. Starlings push birds out of their nests. Then they use the nests themselves. In serious cases, native birds can die out. Losing native birds is bad for habitats.

## BROOD PARASITES

**Brood parasites trick other birds into raising their babies. They lay eggs in the other birds' nests. The other birds care for the eggs until they hatch. Young brood parasites sometimes push the other eggs out of the nest.**

Young brood parasites may take other chicks' food. The original chicks sometimes starve.

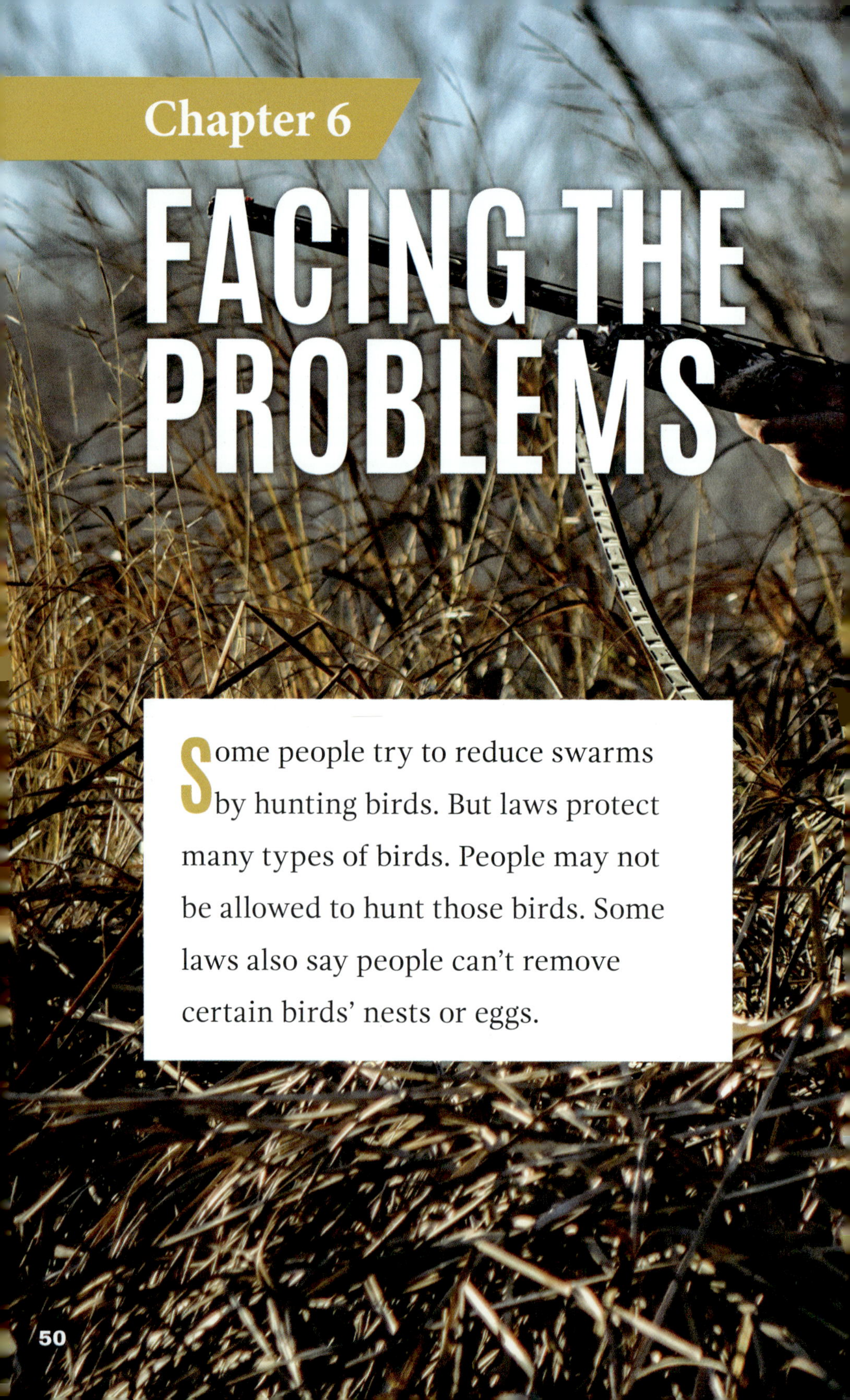

Chapter 6

# FACING THE PROBLEMS

Some people try to reduce swarms by hunting birds. But laws protect many types of birds. People may not be allowed to hunt those birds. Some laws also say people can't remove certain birds' nests or eggs.

Laws in some areas state where or when people can hunt birds.

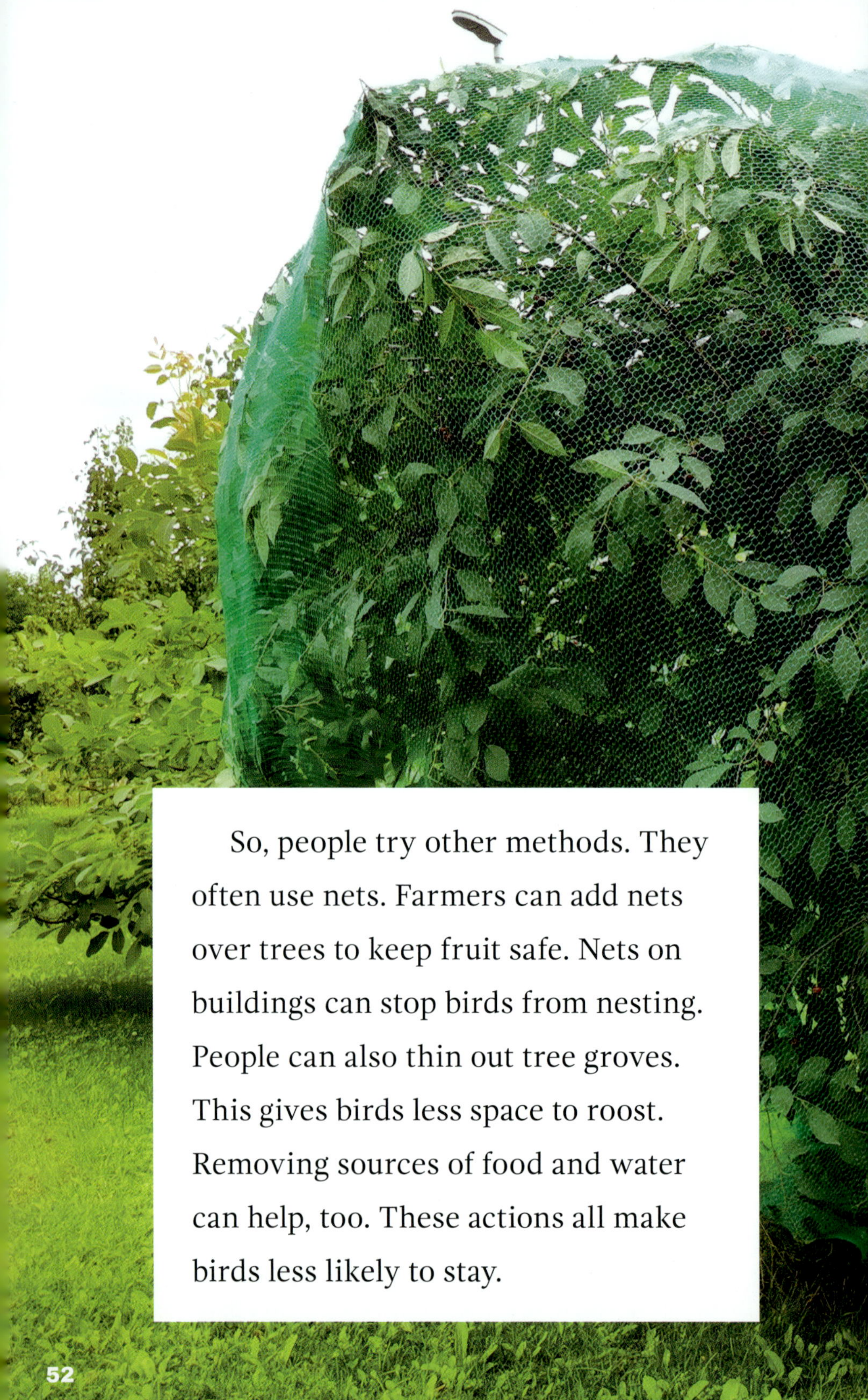

So, people try other methods. They often use nets. Farmers can add nets over trees to keep fruit safe. Nets on buildings can stop birds from nesting. People can also thin out tree groves. This gives birds less space to roost. Removing sources of food and water can help, too. These actions all make birds less likely to stay.

Tree nets can keep birds away without hurting the trees or the birds.

## COCKATOOS

In 2021, cockatoos swarmed Nowra, a town in Australia. Cockatoos are noisy. They pull up crops. They chew on furniture and buildings. Laws protect them. So, people can't hunt them or chase them away. People have to wait for the birds to leave.

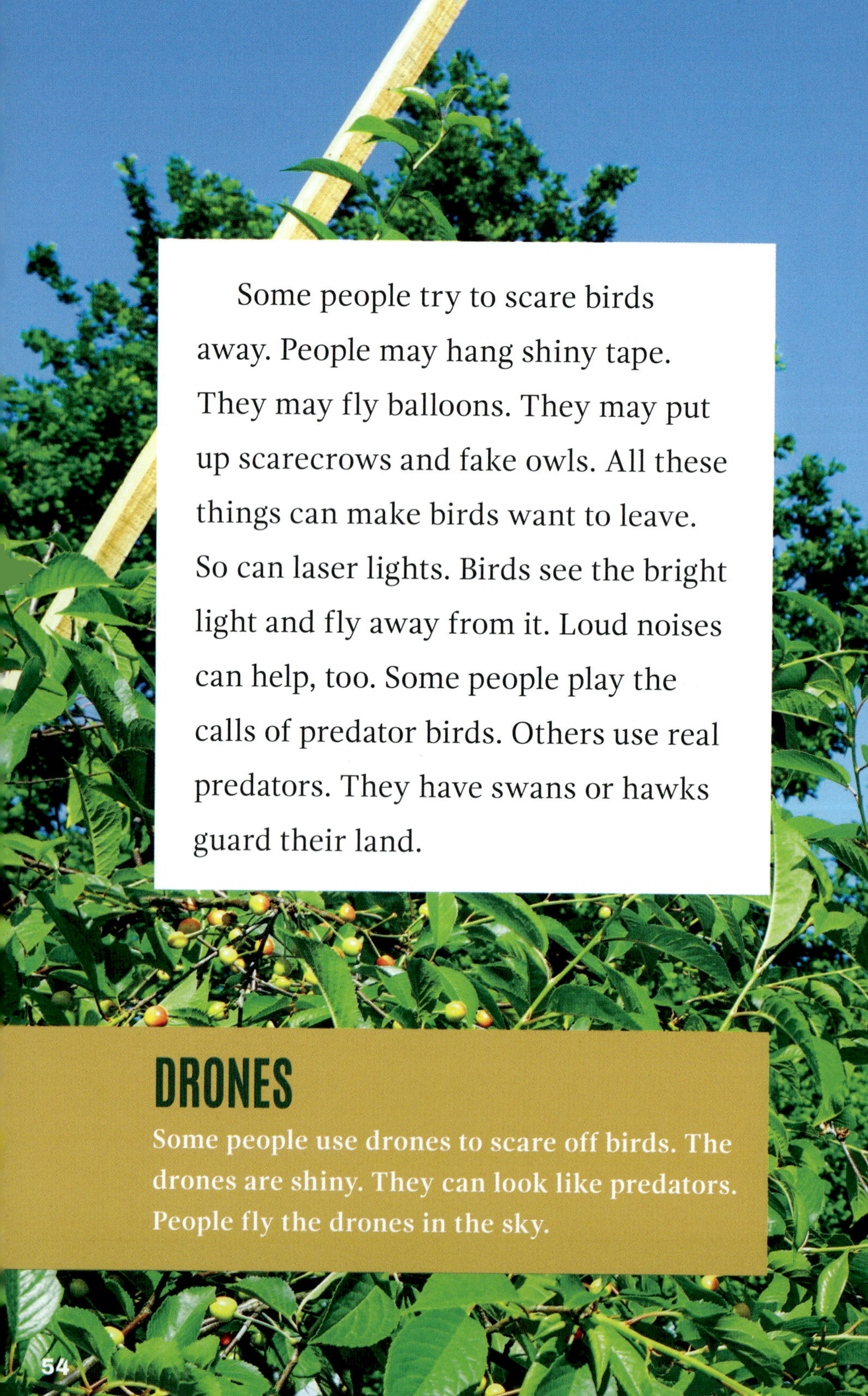

Some people try to scare birds away. People may hang shiny tape. They may fly balloons. They may put up scarecrows and fake owls. All these things can make birds want to leave. So can laser lights. Birds see the bright light and fly away from it. Loud noises can help, too. Some people play the calls of predator birds. Others use real predators. They have swans or hawks guard their land.

## DRONES

Some people use drones to scare off birds. The drones are shiny. They can look like predators. People fly the drones in the sky.

People may place cutouts of predator birds near plants or windows.

In the United States, up to one billion birds die each year from flying into windows.

Many birds are smart. They can get used to changes. So, people keep trying new ideas. For example, one idea tries to limit the number of pigeons. People add a chemical to bird feed. A machine releases the feed for pigeons. The chemical doesn't hurt the pigeons. But it stops their eggs from hatching.

## NEW GLASS

**Birds often crash into glass buildings. This hurts birds and costs people money. Many people and companies mark their glass. They add stickers or give the glass patterns. That way, birds can see the glass more easily.**

# MAP

1. California, United States: Sooty shearwaters and swifts invade towns.
2. Montana, United States: Ravens roost on electrical lines and cause power failures.
3. New York, United States: A plane makes an emergency landing on the Hudson River due to a bird strike.

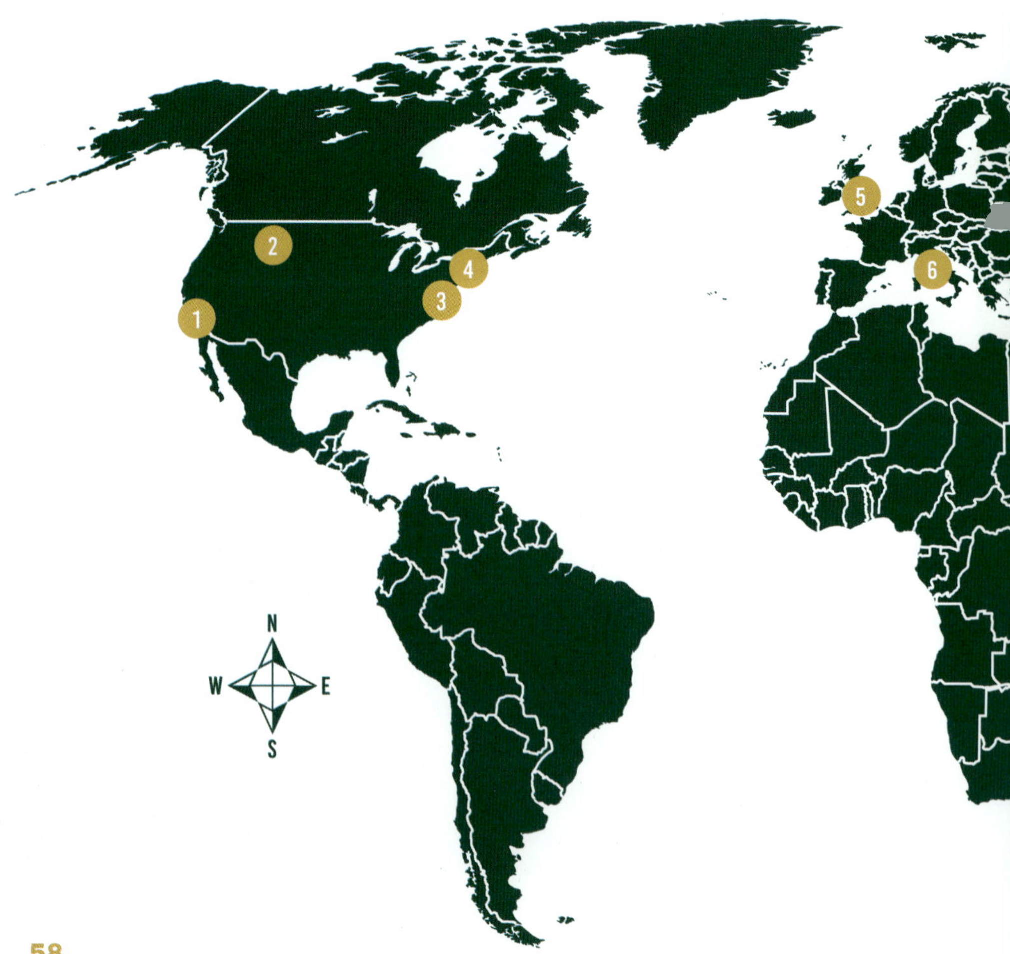

4. Boston, United States: 62 people die in the worst bird strike in history.
5. London, England: A new law bans people from feeding pigeons in Trafalgar Square.
6. Rome, Italy: Starling poop rains down and causes traffic problems.
7. Delhi, India: Black kites swarm the city, attracted to waste from meat-cleaning factories.
8. Nowra, Australia: Thousands of cockatoos invade a town.

# COMPREHENSION QUESTIONS

*Write your answers on a separate piece of paper.*

1. Write a few sentences explaining the main ideas of Chapter 2.
2. Which method for stopping bird swarms do you think is the best idea? Why?
3. When and where was the worst bird strike in history?
   - A. Alaska, 1995
   - B. Boston, 1960
   - C. New York, 2009
4. How could drones keep birds away from an area?
   - A. Drones can scare the birds away.
   - B. Drones can kill the birds.
   - C. Drones can take pictures of the birds.

5. What does **adapt** mean in this book?

*So, some birds stay permanently. They* ***adapt*** *to city life. They find new food sources. They find material for nests.*

A. to change to fit a new place
B. to be uncomfortable somewhere
C. to find food easily

6. What does **recover** mean in this book?

*Another common illness is histoplasmosis. Many people* ***recover*** *if they get it. But others die.*

A. to hate birds
B. to get better
C. to clean germs

*Answer key on page 64.*

# GLOSSARY

**crops**
Plants that people grow for food.

**deter**
To stop something or make it hard to do.

**drones**
Aircraft that people control from far away or that fly on their own.

**engines**
Parts of machines that help them move.

**habitats**
The places where animals normally live.

**invasive**
Spreading quickly in a new area and causing many problems there.

**migrate**
To move from one region to another.

**native**
Originally living in an area.

**pollution**
Things that are dirty or unsafe.

**predators**
Animals that hunt and eat other animals.

**radar**
A system that sends out radio waves to locate objects.

**species**
Groups of animals or plants that are similar and can breed with one another.

# TO LEARN MORE

## BOOKS

Breach, Jen. *Bird Migration*. Mendota Heights, MN: Focus Readers, 2024.

Debbink, Andrea. *Birds of Prey*. Minneapolis: Abdo Publishing, 2023.

Gendell, Megan. *Hawks*. Mendota Heights, MN: Apex Editions, 2022.

## ONLINE RESOURCES

Visit **www.apexeditions.com** to find links and resources related to this title.

# ABOUT THE AUTHOR

Heather Rook Bylenga lives in the Pacific Northwest with her family. Outdoors, she can be found hiking or running. Indoors, she can be found curled up on her couch with a book and a cup of tea.

# INDEX

airports, 4, 26

bird strikes, 18, 20, 22, 24, 26
blackbirds, 43
black kites, 29
blue jays, 48
Boston, United States, 20

Canada geese, 20, 22, 23
cockatoos, 53
cowbirds, 43
crows, 43

Delhi, India, 29
drones, 54
droppings, 32, 35, 37, 42, 44, 47

glass, 57
grackles, 41
gulls, 26

habitats, 13, 48
hawks, 38, 54
hunting, 50, 53

lapwings, 7
London, England, 38

migrating, 10, 13, 30–31, 37
Montana, United States, 44

New York, United States, 15, 22
Nowra, Australia, 53

pigeons, 15, 38, 47, 57
pilots, 6, 22–23
planes, 4, 6–7, 18, 20, 22, 24
pollution, 47

ravens, 44
Rome, Italy, 37

Salt Lake City, United States, 26
snowy owls, 26
sooty shearwaters, 16
sparrows, 15
starlings, 4, 7, 15, 20, 37, 41, 44, 48
swifts, 31

## ANSWER KEY:

1. Answers will vary; 2. Answers will vary; 3. B; 4. A; 5. A; 6. B